Ninja Foodi Smart XL Grill Cookbook 2021

BY KIM AZUMI

CONTENTS

Chapter 1: Breakfast

Sweet BBQ Chicken Meal

(Prepping time: 5-10 minutes\ Cooking time: 40 minutes |For 4 servings)

Ingredients

- Salt and pepper to taste
- 1 cup white vinegar
- ¾ cup onion, chopped
- ¼ cup tomato paste
- ¼ cup garlic, minced
- 1 cup of water
- 1 cup of soy sauce
- ¾ cup of sugar
- 6 chicken drumsticks

Directions

1. Take a Ziploc bag and add all ingredients to it

2. Marinate for at least 2 hours in your refrigerator

3. Insert the crisper basket, and close the hood

4. Preheat Ninja Foodi Smart XL by pressing the "AIR CRISP" option at 390 degrees F for 40 minutes

5. Place the grill pan accessory in the air fryer

6. Flip the chicken after every 10 minutes

7. Take a saucepan and pour the marinade into it, and heat over medium flame until sauce thickens

8. Brush with the glaze

9. Serve warm and enjoy!

<u>Nutrition Values (Per Serving)</u>

- Calories: 460
- Fat: 20 g
- Saturated Fat: 5 g
- Carbohydrates: 26 g
- Fiber: 3 g
- Sodium: 126 mg
- Protein: 28 g

Awesome Tater Tots Eggs

(Prepping time: 5-10 minutes\ Cooking time: 25 minutes |For 4 servings)

Ingredients

- 1 pound frozen tater tots
- 1 cup cheddar cheese, shredded
- 2 sausages, cooked and sliced
- Cooking spray as needed
- Salt and pepper to taste
- ¼ cup milk
- 5 whole eggs

Directions

1. Preheat your Ninja Foodi Smart XL in Bake mode at 390 degrees F for 3 minutes

2. Take a bowl and add eggs, milk, season with salt and pepper

3. Take a small baking pan and grease with oil

4. Add egg mix to the pan and transfer to your Foodi

5. Cook for 5 minutes, place sausages on top of eggs, sprinkle cheese on top

6. Bake for 20 minutes more

7. Serve and enjoy!

Nutrition Values (Per Serving)

- Calories: 187
- Fat: 8 g
- Saturated Fat: 3 g
- Carbohydrates: 21 g
- Fiber: 1 g
- Sodium: 338 mg
- Protein: 9 g

French Morning Toasties

(Prepping time: 5-10 minutes\ Cooking time: 10 minutes |For 4 servings)

Ingredients

- Cooking spray as needed
- 6 slices bread, sliced into strips
- ¼ teaspoon vanilla extract
- ¼ teaspoon ground cinnamon
- ¼ cup granulated sugar
- ½ cup milk
- 4 whole eggs

Directions

1. Take a bowl and beat in eggs, milk

2. Stir in sugar, vanilla, and cinnamon

3. Dip the bread in the mix

4. Preheat your Ninja Foodi Smart XL in AIR CRISP for 10 minutes at 400 degrees F

5. Transfer bread to the Foodi and cook for 3-5 minutes per side

6. Enjoy!

Nutrition Values (Per Serving)

- Calories: 183
- Fat: 6 g

- Saturated Fat: 2 g
- Carbohydrates: 24 g
- Fiber: 3 g
- Sodium: 269 mg
- Protein: 9 g

Juicy Stuffed Bell Peppers

(Prepping time: 10 minutes\ Cooking time:15 minutes |For 4 servings)

Ingredients

- 4 slices bacon, cooked and chopped
- 4 large eggs
- 1 cup cheddar cheese, shredded
- 4 bell peppers, seeded and tops removed
- Chopped parsley for garnish
- Salt and pepper to taste

Directions

1. Divide cheese and bacon equally and stuff into your bell pepper

2. Add eggs into each bell pepper

3. Season with salt and pepper

4. Pre-heat your Ninja Foodi by pressing the "AIR CRISP" option and setting it to "390 Degrees F."

5. Set the timer to 15 minutes

6. Let it pre-heat until you hear a beep

7. Transfer bell pepper to your cooking basket and transfer to Ninja Foodi Grill

8. Lock lid and cook for 10-15 minutes

9. Cook until egg whites are cooked well until the yolks are slightly runny

10. Remove peppers from the basket and garnish with parsley

11. Serve and enjoy!

Nutrition Values (Per Serving)

- Calories: 326
- Fat: 23 g
- Saturated Fat: 10 g
- Carbohydrates: 10 g
- Fiber: 2 g
- Sodium: 781 mg
- Protein: 22 g

Energetic Bagel Platter

(Prepping time: 5-10 minutes\ Cooking time:8 minutes |For 4 servings)

Ingredients

- 4 bagels, halved
- 2 tablespoons coconut flakes
- 1 cup fine sugar
- 2 tablespoons black coffee, prepared and cooled down
- ¼ cup of coconut milk

Directions

1. Take your Ninja Foodi Grill and open the lid

2. Arrange grill grate and close top

3. Pre-heat Ninja Foodi by pressing the "GRILL" option and setting it to "MEDIUM."

4. Set the timer to 8 minutes

5. Let it pre-heat until you hear a beep

6. Arrange bagels over grill grate and lock lid

7. Cook for 2 minutes

8. Flip sausages and cook for 2 minutes more

9. Repeat the same procedure to Grill remaining Bagels

10. Take a mixing bowl and mix the remaining ingredients

11. Pour the sauce over grilled bagels

12. Serve and enjoy!

Nutrition Values (Per Serving)

- Calories: 300
- Fat: 23 g
- Saturated Fat: 12 g
- Carbohydrates: 42 g
- Fiber: 4 g
- Sodium: 340 mg
- Protein: 18 g

Mushroom Pepper Meal

(Prepping time: 10 minutes\ Cooking time:10 minutes |For 4 servings)

Ingredients

- 4 cremini mushrooms, sliced
- 4 large eggs
- ½ cup cheddar cheese, shredded
- ½ onion, chopped
- ¼ cup whole milk
- Sea salt
- ½ bell pepper, seeded and diced
- Black pepper

Directions

1. Add eggs and milk into a medium bowl
2. Whisk them together
3. Add mushrooms, onion, bell pepper, and cheese
4. Mix them well
5. Preheat by selecting the "BAKE" option and setting it to 400 degrees F
6. Set the timer for 10 minutes
7. Pour the egg mixture into the baking pan and spread evenly
8. Let it pre-heat until you hear a beep
9. Then close the lid

10. Cook for 10 minutes

11. Serve and enjoy!

<u>Nutrition Values (Per Serving)</u>

- Calories: 153
- Fat: 10 g
- Saturated Fat: 2 g
- Carbohydrates: 5 g
- Fiber: 1 g
- Sodium: 494 mg
- Protein: 11 g

Bacon Bombs

Prep Time: 5 min

Cooking Time: 7 min

Number of Servings: 4

Ingredients:

3 large eggs, lightly beaten

4-ounces whole-wheat pizza dough, freshly prepared

Cooking spray

3 bacon slices, crisped and crumbled

1-ounce cream cheese softened

1 tablespoon fresh chives, chopped

Directions:

1. Press the "Bake" button on the Ninja Foodi Smart XL Grill and adjust the time for 16 minutes at 350 degrees F.
2. Crack eggs in a non-stick pan and stir fry for 1 minute.
3. Stir in the bacon, chives, and cream cheese and keep aside.
4. Cut the pizza dough into 4 equal pieces and roll each into circles.
5. Put ¼ of the bacon-egg mixture in the center of the dough circle and seal the edges with water.
6. Place the doughs in the Ninja Foodi when it shows "Add Food" and spray them with cooking oil.
7. Bake for 6 minutes and dish out to serve warm.

Nutritional Values (Per Serving):

Calories: 284
Fat: 7.9g
Saturated Fat: 0g

Carbohydrates: 46g
Fiber: 3.6g
Sodium: 704mg
Protein: 7.9g

Breakfast Pockets

Prep Time: 5 min

Cooking Time: 11 min

Number of Servings: 6

Ingredients:

1 box puff pastry sheets

5 eggs

½ cup sausage crumbles, cooked

½ cup bacon, cooked

½ cup cheddar cheese, shredded

Directions:

1. Press the "Bake" button on the Ninja Foodi Smart XL Grill and adjust the time for 10 minutes at 370 degrees F.
2. Crack eggs in a non-stick pan and stir fry for 1 minute.
3. Stir in the bacon and sausages and keep aside.
4. Cut the puff pastry into equal-sized rectangles and add a scoop of egg mixture and cheese in the center.
5. Seal the edges with water and transfer into the Ninja Foodi when it shows "Add Food."
6. Spray them with cooking oil and bake for 10 minutes.
7. Dish out in a platter and serve warm.

Nutritional Values (Per Serving):

Calories: 387
Fat: 6g
Saturated Fat: 9.9g
Carbohydrates: 41g
Fiber: 2.9g
Sodium: 154mg
Protein: 6.6g

Avocado Flautas

Prep Time: 5 min

Cooking Time: 15 min

Number of Servings: 8

Ingredients:

8 eggs, beaten

1 tablespoon butter

½ teaspoon salt

1½ teaspoons cumin

8 fajita size tortillas

8 bacon slices, cooked

½ cup feta cheese, crumbled

¼ teaspoon pepper

1 teaspoon chili powder

4 oz cream cheese, softened

½ cup Mexican cheese, shredded

AVOCADO CRÈME

½ cup sour cream

½ teaspoon salt

2 small avocados

1 lime, juiced

¼ teaspoon black pepper

Directions:

1. Press the "Air Crisp" button on the Ninja Foodi Smart XL Grill and adjust the time for 10 minutes at 400 degrees F.

2. Put butter in a skillet on medium heat and add eggs.
3. Stir fry for 3 minutes and add salt, chili powder, pepper, and cumin.
4. Spread cream cheese on the tortillas and place bacon pieces over them.
5. Top with egg mixture and shredded cheese.
6. Tightly roll each tortilla and place them in the Ninja Foodi when it shows "Add Food".
7. Air crisp for 12 minutes, flipping halfway through.
8. Put the avocado crème ingredients in a blender and process until smooth.
9. Dish out the baked flautas in a platter and serve warm with avocado cheese and cotija cheese.

Nutritional Values (Per Serving):

Calories: 212
Fat: 11.8g
Saturated Fat: 2.2g
Carbohydrates: 14.6g
Fiber: 4.4g
Sodium: 321mg
Protein: 17.3g

Classic French Burrito

(Prepping time: 5-10 minutes\ Cooking time: 5 minutes |For 2 servings)

Ingredients

- 2 tortillas
- ½ cup bacon, cooked crisp and crumbled
- ½ cup cheddar cheese, shredded
- 2 whole eggs, scrambled

Directions

1. Take a bowl and add eggs, bacon, and cheese
2. Top tortillas with the mix
3. Roll the tortillas, transfer to the Ninja Foodi Smart XL
4. Select AIR CRISP and cook for 5 minutes at 250 degrees F
5. Serve and enjoy!

Nutrition Values (Per Serving)

- Calories: 531
- Fat: 15 g
- Saturated Fat: 3 g
- Carbohydrates: 81 g
- Fiber: 2 g
- Sodium: 1125 mg
- Protein: 18 g

Chapter 2: Vegetarian And Vegan Recipes

Feisty Avocado Toast

(Prepping time: 5-10 minutes\ Cooking time: 5 minutes |For 2 servings)

Ingredients

- ¼ cup tomato, chopped
- 2 slices bread
- Salt to taste
- 1 teaspoon lemon juice
- 1 garlic clove, minced
- 1 avocado, mashed

Directions

1. Take a bowl and add avocado, lemon juice, garlic, salt, and pepper

2. Spread the mix over bread slices

3. Sprinkle tomato on top

4. Transfer to the Ninja Foodi Smart XL and grill for 2-3 minutes at 350 degrees F on GRILL mode

5. Serve and enjoy!

Nutrition Values (Per Serving)

- Calories: 226
- Fat: 15 g

- Saturated Fat: 3 g
- Carbohydrates: 21 g
- Fiber: 2 g
- Sodium: 267 mg
- Protein: 5 g

Mexican Corn Dish

(Prepping time: 5-10 minutes\ Cooking time: 12 minutes |For 4 servings)

Ingredients

- 2 tablespoons lime juice
- ½ cup mayonnaise
- ½ cup sour cream
- 2 teaspoons garlic powder
- 2 teaspoons onion powder
- 1 and ¼ cups Cotija cheese, crumbled
- Salt and pepper to taste
- 3 tablespoons canola oil
- 6 ears corn

Directions

1. Set your Ninja Foodi Smart XL to grill mode, set temperature to MAX, and timer to 12 minutes

2. Let it preheat until you hear a beep

3. Brush the corn ears with oil, season with salt and pepper

4. Transfer to grill and cook for 6 minutes per side

5. Take a bowl and mix in the remaining ingredients; mix well

6. Cover corn mix and serve

7. Enjoy!

Nutrition Values (Per Serving)

- Calories: 156
- Fat: 10 g
- Saturated Fat: 3 g
- Carbohydrates: 15 g
- Fiber: 3 g
- Sodium: 163 mg
- Protein: 6 g

Crispy Brussels

(Prepping time: 5-10 minutes\ Cooking time:12 minutes |For 4 servings)

Ingredients

- 1 pound brussels sprouts, halved
- 6 slices bacon, chopped
- 2 tablespoons olive oil, extra virgin
- 1 teaspoon salt
- ½ teaspoon ground black pepper

Directions

1. Add Brussels, bacon, olive oil, salt, and pepper into a mixing bowl

2. Pre-heat Ninja Foodi by pressing the "AIR CRISP" option and setting it to "390 degrees F."

3. Set the timer to 12 minutes

4. Let it pre-heat until you hear a beep

5. Arrange Brussels over basket and lock lid

6. Cook for 6 minutes

7. Shake it generously and cook for 6 minutes more

8. Serve and enjoy!

Nutrition Values (Per Serving)

- Calories: 279
- Fat: 18 g

- Saturated Fat: 4 g
- Carbohydrates: 12 g
- Fiber: 4 g
- Sodium: 874 mg
- Protein: 14 g

Honey-Licious Asparagus

(Prepping time: 5-10 minutes\ Cooking time:15 minutes |For 4 servings)

Ingredients

- 2 pounds asparagus, trimmed
- 4 tablespoons tarragon, minced
- ¼ cup honey
- 2 tablespoons olive oil
- 1 teaspoon salt
- ½ teaspoon pepper

Directions

1. Add asparagus, oil, salt, honey, pepper, tarragon into a mixing bowl

2. Toss them well

3. Pre-heat Ninja Foodi by pressing the "GRILL" option and setting it to "MED."

4. Set the timer to 8 minutes

5. Let it pre-heat until you hear a beep

6. Arrange asparagus over grill grate and lock lid

7. Cook for 4 minutes

8. Flip the asparagus and cook for 4 minutes more

9. Serve and enjoy!

<u>Nutrition Values (Per Serving)</u>

- Calories: 240
- Fat: 15 g
- Saturated Fat: 3 g
- Carbohydrates: 31 g
- Fiber: 1 g
- Sodium: 103 mg
- Protein: 7 g

Well Prepped Yogurt Broccoli

(Prepping time: 5-10 minutes\ Cooking time:10 minutes |For 2 servings)

Ingredients

- 1 pound broccoli, cut into florets
- 2 tablespoons yogurt
- ¼ teaspoon turmeric powder
- 1 tablespoon chickpea flour
- ¼ teaspoon spice mix
- ½ teaspoon salt
- ½ teaspoon red chili powder

Directions

1. Wash the broccoli florets thoroughly
2. Add all ingredients except florets into a mixing bowl
3. Mix them well
4. Add florets to the mix
5. Let them sit in the fridge for 30 minutes
6. Take your Ninja Foodi Grill and open the lid
7. Arrange grill grate and close top
8. Pre-heat Ninja Foodi by pressing the "AIR CRISP" option and setting it to "390 Degrees F
9. Set the timer to 10 minutes
10. Let it pre-heat until you hear a beep

11. Arrange florets over the Grill Basket and lock the lid

12. Cook for 10 minutes

13. Serve and enjoy!

Nutrition Values (Per Serving)

- Calories: 113
- Fat: 2 g
- Saturated Fat: 0 g
- Carbohydrates: 12 g
- Fiber: 4 g
- Sodium: 124 mg
- Protein: 07 g

Fancy Asparagus And Roasted Potatoes

(Prepping time: 5-10 minutes\ Cooking time: 10 minutes |For 4 servings)

Ingredients

- Salt and pepper to taste
- 1 teaspoon dried dill
- 4 potatoes, diced and boiled
- 2 stalks scallions, chopped
- 1 tablespoon olive oil
- 1 pound asparagus, trimmed and sliced

Directions

1. Take the asparagus and coat with oil

2. Season well with scallions

3. Set your Ninja Foodi Smart XL to AIR CRISP mode and set the temperature to 350 degrees F; set timer to 5 minutes

4. Once done, transfer asparagus to the cooking basket, cook for 5 minutes

5. Transfer to a bowl

6. Stir in remaining ingredients and mix well

7. Serve and enjoy!

Nutrition Values (Per Serving)

- Calories: 222
- Fat: 8 g
- Saturated Fat: 3 g
- Carbohydrates: 36 g
- Fiber: 3 g
- Sodium: 779 mg
- Protein: 6 g

Lemon Pepper Brussels Sprouts

(Prepping time: 5-10 minutes\ Cooking time: 10 minutes |For 4 servings)

Ingredients

- Salt to taste
- 2 teaspoons lemon pepper seasoning
- 2 tablespoons olive oil
- 1 pound brussels sprouts, sliced

Directions

1. Take your Brussels and coat them with oil

2. Season the sprouts with salt and lemon pepper

3. Spread the prepared Brussels over the Cooking basket

4. Select the broil option, with the temperature set to 350 degrees F and timer set to 5 minutes

5. Let it cook, serve, and enjoy!

Nutrition Values (Per Serving)

- Calories: 229
- Fat: 18 g
- Saturated Fat: 2 g
- Carbohydrates: 12 g
- Fiber: 2 g
- Sodium: 360 mg
- Protein: 8 g

Chapter 3: Chicken And Poultry Recipes

Lovely Lemon Mustard Chicken

(Prepping time: 5-10 minutes\ Cooking time: 30 minutes |For 6 servings)

Ingredients

- 6 chicken thighs
- Salt and pepper to taste
- 3 teaspoons dried Italian seasoning
- 1 tablespoon oregano, dried
- ½ cup Dijon mustard
- ¼ cup of vegetable oil
- 2 tablespoons lemon juice

Directions

1. Take a bowl and add all listed ingredients except chicken

2. Mix everything well

3. Brush both sides of the chicken with the mixture, transfer chicken to the cooking basket

4. Set your Ninja Foodi Smart XL to roast mode, set temperature to 350 degrees F

5. Select chicken mode and start; let it cook until the timer runs out

6. Serve and enjoy!

Nutrition Values (Per Serving)

- Calories: 797
- Fat: 52 g
- Saturated Fat: 20 g
- Carbohydrates: 45 g
- Fiber: 9 g
- Sodium: 1566 mg
- Protein: 42 g

Sesame Chicken Breast

Prep Time: 5 min

Cooking Time: 20 min

Number of Servings: 2

Ingredients:

2 tablespoons sesame oil

2 chicken breasts

1 teaspoon kosher salt

½ teaspoon black pepper

¼ teaspoon cayenne pepper

1 tablespoon onions powder

1 tablespoon sweet paprika

1 tablespoon garlic powder

Directions:

1. Press the "Bake" button on the Ninja Foodi Smart XL Grill and adjust the time for 20 minutes at 380 degrees F.
2. Season the chicken breasts with sesame oil and all other spices.
3. Place the chicken in the Ninja Foodi when it shows "Add Food".
4. Bake for about 20 minutes and dish out to serve warm.

Nutritional Values (Per Serving):

Calories: 453
Fat: 2.4g
Saturated Fat: 3g
Carbohydrates: 18g
Fiber: 2.3g
Sodium: 216mg
Protein: 23.2g

Lemon Pepper Chicken

Prep Time: 5 min

Cooking Time: 20 min

Number of Servings: 4

Ingredients:

1 tablespoon lemon pepper

4 boneless skinless chicken breasts

1 teaspoon table salt

1½ teaspoons granulated garlic

Directions:

1. Press the "Grill" button on the Ninja Foodi Smart XL Grill and adjust the time for 20 minutes at Medium.
2. Season the chicken breasts with salt, granulated garlic, and lemon pepper.
3. Place the chicken in the Ninja Foodi when it shows "Add Food."
4. Grill for about 20 minutes, flipping halfway through.
5. Dish out in a platter and serve warm.

Nutritional Values (Per Serving):

Calories: 284
Fat: 25g
Saturated Fat: 1g
Carbohydrates: 35g
Fiber: 2g
Sodium: 460mg
Protein: 26g

Chicken Broccoli

Prep Time: 5 min

Cooking Time: 20 min

Number of Servings: 4

Ingredients:

1 tablespoon olive oil

1 pound chicken breast, boneless and cut into bite-sized pieces

½ pound broccoli, cut into small florets

1 tablespoon soy sauce, low sodium

2 teaspoons hot sauce

Black pepper, to taste

½ onion, sliced

½ teaspoon garlic powder

1 tablespoon fresh minced ginger

1 teaspoon sesame seed oil

2 teaspoons rice vinegar

Salt, to taste

Directions:

1. Press the "Grill" button on the Ninja Foodi Smart XL Grill and adjust the time for 20 minutes at Medium.
2. Combine the chicken breasts with onion and broccoli in a bowl.
3. Toss in the remaining ingredients and mix thoroughly.
4. Place the chicken in the Ninja Foodi when it shows "Add Food."
5. Grill for about 20 minutes, flipping halfway through.
6. Dish out in a platter and top with lemon juice to serve.

Nutritional Values (Per Serving):

Calories: 352
Fat: 14g
Saturated Fat: 2g
Carbohydrates: 5.8g
Fiber: 0g
Sodium: 220mg
Protein: 26g

Sweet Tangy Orange Chicken

(Prepping time: 5-10 minutes\ Cooking time: 15 minutes |For 4 servings)

Ingredients

- 2 teaspoons ground coriander
- ½ teaspoons garlic salt
- ¼ teaspoon ground black pepper
- 12 chicken wings
- 1 tablespoon canola oil
- ¼ cup butter, melted
- 3 tablespoons honey
- ½ cup of orange juice
- 1/3 cup Sriracha chili sauce
- 2 tablespoons lime juice
- ¼ cup cilantro, chopped

Directions

1. Take the chicken and coat them well with oil
2. Season with spices, let them sit for 2 hours in the fridge
3. Add remaining ingredients to a saucepan and cook over low heat for 3-4 minutes
4. Set your Ninja Foodi Smart XL to GRILI and MED mode
5. Set timer to 10 minutes

6. Add chicken to grill grate, cook for 5 minutes, flip and cook for 5 minutes more

7. Serve and enjoy once done!

Nutrition Values (Per Serving)

- Calories: 320
- Fat: 14 g
- Saturated Fat: 4 g
- Carbohydrates: 19 g
- Fiber: 1 g
- Sodium: 258 mg
- Protein: 25 g

Fancy Turkey Bacon Roast

(Prepping time: 5-10 minutes\ Cooking time:20 minutes |For 6 servings)

Ingredients

- 8 pieces (6 ounces each) turkey cutlets
- 8 ham slices
- 4 tablespoons sage leaves
- 2 tablespoons butter, melted
- Pepper and salt to taste

Directions

1. Take your turkey cutlets into a bowl and season with salt and pepper
2. Wrap them with bacon
3. Brush with butter and add sage leaves on top
4. Take your baking pan and generously grease with butter
5. Pre-heat Ninja Foodi by pressing the "BAKE" option and setting it to "350-degree F."
6. Set the timer to 20 minutes
7. Let it pre-heat until you hear a beep
8. Arrange cutlets in a baking pan and transfer to Grill
9. Cook for 20 minutes
10. Serve and enjoy!

Nutrition Values (Per Serving)

- Calories: 450

- Fat: 20 g

- Saturated Fat: 4 g

- Carbohydrates: 2 g

- Fiber: 0.5 g

- Sodium: 656 mg

- Protein: 51 g

Juicy BBQ Chicken

(Prepping time: 5-10 minutes\ Cooking time:12 minutes |For 4 servings)

Ingredients

- 6 chicken drumsticks
- ½ tablespoon Worcestershire sauce
- 2 teaspoons BBQ seasoning
- 1 tablespoon brown sugar
- 1 teaspoon dried onion, chopped
- 1/3 cup spice seasoning
- 1 tablespoon bourbon
- 1 pinch teaspoon salt
- ½ cup ketchup

Directions

1. Add all ingredients into a saucepan except drumsticks

2. Stir cook for 8-10 minutes

3. Keep them aside and let it cool

4. Pre-heat Ninja Foodi by pressing the "GRILL" option and setting it to "MED."

5. Set the timer to 12 minutes

6. Let it pre-heat until you hear a beep

7. Arrange drumsticks over grill grate, brush with remaining sauce

8. Lock lid and cook for 6 minutes

9. flip and brush with more sauce

10. Cook for 6 minutes more

11. Serve and enjoy!

Nutrition Values (Per Serving)

- Calories: 300
- Fat: 8 g
- Saturated Fat: 1 g
- Carbohydrates: 10 g
- Fiber: 1.5 g
- Sodium: 319 mg
- Protein: 12.5 g

Grilled Orange Chicken

(Prepping time: 5-10 minutes\ Cooking time:15 minutes |For 4 servings)

Ingredients

- 12 chicken wings
- ½ cup of orange juice
- 2 teaspoons ground coriander
- 1 tablespoon canola oil
- ¼ cup butter, melted
- 3 tablespoons honey
- 1/3 cup Sriracha chili sauce
- 2 tablespoons lime juice
- ¼ cup cilantro, chopped
- ½ teaspoon garlic salt
- ¼ teaspoon ground black pepper

Directions

1. Take your chicken into a bowl

2. Coat the chicken with oil, season with spices

3. Let it chill for 2 hours

4. Add listed ingredients and keep it on the side

5. Cook for 3-4 minutes in a saucepan

6. Pre-heat Ninja Foodi by pressing the "GRILL" option and setting it to "MED."

7. Set the timer to 10 minutes

8. Let it pre-heat until you hear a beep

9. Arrange chicken over the grill grate

10. Cook for 5 minutes

11. Flip and let it cook for 5 minutes more

12. Serve with sauce on top

13. Enjoy!

Nutrition Values (Per Serving)

- Calories: 320
- Fat: 14 g
- Saturated Fat: 4 g
- Carbohydrates: 19 g
- Fiber: 1 g
- Sodium: 258 mg
- Protein: 25 g

Clean Apple Flavored Alfredo Chicken

(Prepping time: 5-10 minutes\ Cooking time: 20 minutes |For 4 servings)

Ingredients

- 1 large apple, wedged
- 1 tablespoon lemon juice
- 4 chicken breast, halved
- 4 teaspoons chicken seasoning
- 4 slices provolone cheese
- ¼ cup blue cheese, crumbled
- ½ cup alfredo sauce

Directions

1. Take a mixing bowl and add seasoning
2. Take another bowl and toss apple with lemon juice
3. Set your Ninja Foodi Smart XL to Grill and MED mode, set timer to 16 minutes
4. Transfer chicken over grill grate, lock lid, and cook for 8 minutes
5. Flip and cook for 8 minutes more
6. Grill the apple in a similar manner, 2 minutes per side
7. Serve the cooked chicken with sauce, grilled apple, and cheese

8. Enjoy!

Nutrition Values (Per Serving)

- Calories: 247
- Fat: 19 g
- Saturated Fat: 3 g
- Carbohydrates: 29 g
- Fiber: 2 g
- Sodium: 850 mg
- Protein: 14 g

Excellent Coconut Touched Chicken Meal

(Prepping time: 5-10 minutes\ Cooking time: 12 minutes |For 4 servings)

Ingredients

- 2 large whole eggs
- 2 teaspoons garlic powder
- 1 teaspoon salt and ½ teaspoon pepper
- ¾ cup coconut minos
- 1 pound chicken tenders
- Cooking spray as needed

Directions

1. Set your Ninja Foodi Smart XL to AIR CRISP mode
2. Set temperature to 400 degrees F and set timer to 12 minutes
3. Take a large baking sheet and grease with cooking spray
4. Take a wide dish, add eggs, garlic, salt, and pepper, whisk well
5. Add almond meal, coconut and mix well
6. Take chicken tenders and dip them in egg mix, dip in coconut mix afterward
7. Shake any excess
8. Transfer the prepared chicken Grill, spray the tenders with a bit of oil
9. Air Fry for about 10-14 minutes until golden, serve and enjoy!

Nutrition Values (Per Serving)

- Calories: 180
- Fat: 1 g
- Saturated Fat: 0 g
- Carbohydrates: 3 g
- Fiber: 1 g
- Sodium: 214 mg
- Protein: 0 g

Chapter 4: Fish And Seafood Recipes

Tuna Patties

Prep Time: 5 min

Cooking Time: 10 min

Number of Servings: 4

Ingredients:

1½ tablespoons almond flour

2 cans tuna, packed in water

1½ tablespoons mayo

1 teaspoon garlic powder

Pinch of salt and pepper

1 teaspoon dried dill

½ teaspoon onion powder

½ lemon, juiced

Directions:

1. Press the "Grill" button on the Ninja Foodi Smart XL Grill and adjust the time for 10 minutes at Medium.
2. Combine all the tuna patties ingredients in a bowl and make equal-sized patties out of this mixture.
3. Place the tuna patties in the Ninja Foodi when it shows "Add Food".
4. Grill for about 10 minutes, tossing the patties halfway through.
5. Dish out the fillets in a platter and serve warm.

Nutritional Values (Per Serving):

Calories: 338
Fat: 3.8g

Saturated Fat: 0.7g
Carbohydrates: 8.3g
Fiber: 2.4g
Sodium: 620mg
Protein: 15.4g

4 Ingredients Catfish

Prep Time: 5 min

Cooking Time: 12 min

Number of Servings: 4

Ingredients:

¼ cup Louisiana fish seasoning

1 tablespoon parsley, chopped

4 catfish fillets

1 tablespoon olive oil

Directions:

1. Press the "Grill" button on the Ninja Foodi Smart XL Grill and adjust the time for 12 minutes at Medium.
2. Combine the catfish fillets with Louisiana fish seasoning in a bowl.
3. Place the fillets in the Ninja Foodi when it shows "Add Food" and spray with olive oil.
4. Grill for about 10 minutes, tossing the patties halfway through.
5. Dish out the fillets in a platter and garnish with parsley to serve.

Nutritional Values (Per Serving):

Calories: 253
Fat: 7.5g
Saturated Fat: 1.1g
Carbohydrates: 10.4g
Fiber: 0g
Sodium: 297mg
Protein: 13.1g

Breaded Shrimp

Prep Time: 5 min

Cooking Time: 16 min

Number of Servings: 4

Ingredients:

2 eggs

1 pound shrimp, peeled and deveined

½ cup panko breadcrumbs

1 teaspoon ginger

1 teaspoon garlic powder

½ cup onion, peeled and diced

1 teaspoon black pepper

Directions:

1. Press the "Air Crisp" button on the Ninja Foodi Smart XL Grill and adjust the time for 16 minutes at 350 degrees F.
2. Combine panko, spices, and onions in one bowl, and whisk eggs in another bowl.
3. Dip the shrimp in the whisked eggs and then dredge in the panko mixture.
4. Place the shrimp in the Ninja Foodi when it shows "Add Food."
5. Grill for about 16 minutes, tossing the patties halfway through.
6. Dish out the fillets in a platter and dish out to serve warm.

Nutritional Values (Per Serving):

Calories: 246
Fat: 7.4g
Saturated Fat: 4.6g
Carbohydrates: 9.4g
Fiber: 2.7g

Sodium: 353mg
Protein: 37.2g

Butter And Garlic Shrimp

(Prepping time: 5-10 minutes\ Cooking time: 5 minutes |For 4 servings)

Ingredients

- 2 garlic cloves, minced
- Salt and pepper to taste
- 1 teaspoon dried parsley
- ½ cup butter, melted
- 1 pound shrimp, peeled and deveined

Directions

1. Take a bowl and add all listed ingredients except shrimp

2. Coat shrimp with the mixture well

3. Transfer to the Air Crisping basket

4. Set your Ninja Foodi Smart XL to Air Crisp mode

5. Air Fry the shrimp for 5 minutes at 400 degrees F

6. Serve and enjoy once done!

Nutrition Values (Per Serving)

- Calories: 159
- Fat: 13 g
- Saturated Fat: 5 g
- Carbohydrates: 3 g
- Fiber: 1 g

- Sodium: 309 mg
- Protein: 8 g

Spicy Buttered Salmon

(Prepping time: 5-10 minutes\ Cooking time:12 minutes |For 4 servings)

Ingredients

- 2 pounds salmon fillets
- 6 tablespoons butter, melted
- 1 and ¼ teaspoon onion salt
- 1 teaspoon dry oregano
- 2 tablespoons lemon pepper
- 1 teaspoon dry basil
- 1 teaspoon ancho chili powder
- Lemon wedges and dill sprigs
- 2 teaspoons cayenne pepper
- 2 teaspoon salt
- 1 teaspoon white pepper, ground
- 1 teaspoon black pepper, ground

Directions

1. Take a mixing bowl and add listed ingredients

2. Season salmon fillets with butter

3. Coat salmon fillets with the mixture

4. Pre-heat Ninja Foodi by pressing the "GRILL" option and setting it to "MED."

5. Set the timer to 10 minutes

6. Let it pre-heat until you hear a beep

7. Arrange prepared fillets over the grill grate

8. cook for 5 minutes

9. then flip and cook for 5 minutes more

10. Serve and enjoy!

Nutrition Values (Per Serving)

- Calories: 300
- Fat: 8 g
- Saturated Fat: 2 g
- Carbohydrates: 17 g
- Fiber: 1 g
- Sodium: 342 mg
- Protein: 26 g

Crispy Crab Patty

(Prepping time: 5-10 minutes\ Cooking time:10 minutes |For 4 servings)

Ingredients

- 12 ounces lump crabmeat
- 1 shallot, minced
- 1 egg, beaten
- 2 tablespoons almond flour
- ¼ cup mayonnaise, low carb
- 2 tablespoons Dijon mustard
- ¼ cup parsley, minced
- 1 lemon, zest
- Pepper and salt as needed

Directions

1. Add all ingredients into a mixing bowl
2. Mix them well
3. Prepare 4 meat from the mixture
4. Pre-heat Ninja Foodi by pressing the "AIR CRISP" option and setting it to "375 Degrees F."
5. Set the timer to 10 minutes
6. Let it pre-heat until you hear a beep
7. Transfer patties to cooking basket
8. Cook for 5 minutes
9. Then flip and cook for 5 minutes more

10. Serve and enjoy!

Nutrition Values (Per Serving)

- Calories: 177
- Fat: 13 g
- Saturated Fat: 2 g
- Carbohydrates: 2.5 g
- Fiber: 0 g
- Sodium: 358 mg
- Protein: 11 g

Paprika Grilled Shrimp

(Prepping time: 5-10 minutes\ Cooking time:6 minutes |For 4 servings)

Ingredients

- 1-pound jumbo shrimps, peeled and deveined
- 2 tablespoons brown sugar
- 1 tablespoon paprika
- 1 tablespoon garlic powder
- 2 tablespoons olive oil
- 1 teaspoon garlic salt
- ½ teaspoon black pepper

Directions

1. Add listed ingredients into a mixing bowl

2. Mix them well

3. Let it chill and marinate for 30-60 minutes

4. Pre-heat Ninja Foodi by pressing the "GRILL" option and setting it to "MED."

5. Set the timer to 6 minutes

6. Let it pre-heat until you hear a beep

7. Arrange prepared shrimps over the grill grate

8. Lock lid and cook for 3 minutes

9. Then flip and cook for 3 minutes more

10. Serve and enjoy!

Nutrition Values (Per Serving)

- Calories: 370
- Fat: 27 g
- Saturated Fat: 3 g
- Carbohydrates: 23 g
- Fiber: 8 g
- Sodium: 182 mg
- Protein: 6 g

Garlic And Salmon Extravaganza

(Prepping time: 10 minutes\ Cooking time: 12 minutes |For 4 servings)

Ingredients

- 2 salmon fillets, 6 ounces each
- 1 teaspoon lemon zest, grated
- ¼ teaspoon fresh rosemary, minced
- ¼ teaspoon salt
- 1 garlic clove, minced
- ¼ teaspoon pepper

Directions

1. Take a bowl and add listed ingredients except for salmon, mix thoroughly
2. Add salmon, let the mixture sit for 15 minutes
3. Set your Ninja Foodi Smart XL to GRILL, MED mode
4. Set timer to 6 minutes
5. Arrange the prepared salmon over the grill grate, lock, and cook for 3 minutes
6. Flip and cook for 3 minutes more
7. Serve once done and enjoy it!

Nutrition Values (Per Serving)

- Calories: 250
- Fat: 8 g
- Saturated Fat: 3g
- Carbohydrates: 22 g
- Fiber: 3 g
- Sodium: 370 mg
- Protein: 36 g

The Cool Haddock Bake

(Prepping time: 10 minutes\ Cooking time: 5-10 minutes |For 4 servings)

Ingredients

- ¼ teaspoon salt
- ¾ cup breadcrumbs
- ¼ cup parmesan cheese, grated
- ¼ teaspoon ground thyme
- ¼ cup butter, melted
- 1 pound haddock fillets
- ¾ cup milk

Directions

1. Take your fish fillets and dredge them well in milk, season with salt and keep them on the side
2. Take a medium-sized mixing bowl, add thyme
3. Add parmesan, cheese, breadcrumbs and mix well
4. Coat the fillets well with the crumb mixture
5. Set your Ninja Foodi Smart XL to BAKE
6. Set temperature to 325 degrees F, set the timer to 13 minutes
7. Transfer to the appliance, cook for 8 minutes
8. Flip and cook for 8 minutes more
9. Enjoy

Nutrition Values (Per Serving)

- Calories: 450
- Fat: 27 g
- Saturated Fat: 12 g
- Carbohydrates: 16 g
- Fiber: 22 g
- Sodium: 1056 mg
- Protein: 44 g

Chapter 5: Beef And Red Meat

Bacon-Wrapped Up Pork Loin

(Prepping time: 5-10 minutes\ Cooking time: 12 minutes |For 4 servings)

Ingredients

- Salt and pepper to taste
- 2 tablespoons vegetable oil
- 4 pork tenderloin fillets
- 8 slices bacon

Directions

1. Take the tenderloin and wrap them with 2 bacon slices, secure with toothpicks

2. Brush all sides with oil

3. Season them with salt and pepper

4. Set your Ninja Foodi Smart XL to GRILL and HIGH, timer to 12 minutes

5. Transfer the prepared meat to the appliance and cook for 6 minutes per side

6. Enjoy!

Nutrition Values (Per Serving)

- Calories: 462

- Fat: 31 g
- Saturated Fat: 8 g
- Carbohydrates: 3 g
- Fiber: 0 g
- Sodium: 610 mg
- Protein: 30 g

Asparagus Steak Tips

Prep Time: 5 min

Cooking Time: 15 min

Number of Servings: 2

Ingredients:

1 lb. steak cubes

1 teaspoon olive oil

½ teaspoon salt

½ teaspoon dried garlic powder

1/8 teaspoon cayenne pepper

½ teaspoon black pepper, freshly ground

½ teaspoon dried onion powder

AIR FRYER ASPARAGUS

¼ teaspoon salt

1 lb. Asparagus, tough ends trimmed

½ teaspoon olive oil

Directions:

1. Press the "Grill" button on the Ninja Foodi Smart XL Grill and adjust the time for 10 minutes at Medium.
2. Combine garlic powder, cayenne pepper, onion powder, salt, and black pepper in a bowl.
3. Place the steak cubes in a Ziploc bag and add garlic powder mixture.
4. Shake the bag well and transfer the steak cubes in the Ninja Foodi when it shows "Add Food."
5. Grill for 10 minutes, tossing the steaks halfway.

6. Season the asparagus with salt and drizzle with olive oil.
7. Add the asparagus into the Ninja Foodi and grill for about 5 minutes.
8. Dish out in a platter and serve warm.

Nutritional Values (Per Serving):

Calories: 361
Fat: 16.3g
Saturated Fat: 4.9g
Carbohydrates: 9.3g
Fiber: 0.1g
Sodium: 515mg
Protein: 33.3g

Korean BBQ Beef

Prep Time: 5 min

Cooking Time: 15 min

Number of Servings: 2

Ingredients:

FOR THE MEAT:

1 lb. Flank steak

Coconut oil spray

¼ cup corn starch

FOR THE SAUCE:

½ cup brown sugar

½ cup soy sauce

2 tablespoons Pompeian white wine vinegar

1 tablespoon hot chili sauce

½ teaspoon sesame seeds

1 teaspoon water

1 clove garlic, crushed

1 teaspoon ground ginger

1 teaspoon cornstarch

Directions:

1. Press the "Grill" button on the Ninja Foodi Smart XL Grill and adjust the time for 10 minutes at Medium.
2. Grease the grill with the coconut oil spray.
3. Dredge the steaks in the cornstarch and transfer into the Ninja Foodi when it shows "Add Food."

4. Combine the rest of the ingredients for the sauce in a pan except cornstarch and water.
5. Whisk cornstarch with water in a bowl and add to the sauce.
6. Cook on medium-low heat until it thickens, and pour the sauce over the steaks to serve.

Nutritional Values (Per Serving):

Calories: 545
Fat: 36.4g
Saturated Fat: 10.1g
Carbohydrates: 0.7g
Fiber: 0.2g
Sodium: 272mg
Protein: 42.5g

Steak and Mushrooms

Prep Time: 5 min

Cooking Time: 10 min

Number of Servings: 4

Ingredients:

1 pound beef sirloin steak, cubed into 1-inch pieces

¼ cup Worcestershire sauce

8-ounces mushrooms, sliced

1 tablespoon olive oil

1 teaspoon parsley flakes

1 teaspoon paprika

1 teaspoon chili flakes, crushed

Directions:

1. Press the "Air Crisp" button on the Ninja Foodi Smart XL Grill and adjust the time for 10 minutes at 400 degrees F.
2. Combine the steak with olive oil, parsley, mushrooms, paprika, chili flakes, and Worcestershire sauce in a bowl.
3. Cover the bowl and marinate the steaks for about 3 hours in the refrigerator.
4. Place the steaks and mushrooms in the Ninja Foodi when it shows "Add Food."
5. Air crisp for about 10 minutes, tossing well in the halfway.
6. Dish out in a platter and serve warm.

Nutritional Values (Per Serving):

Calories: 405
Fat: 22.7g

Saturated Fat: 6.1g
Carbohydrates: 6.1g
Fiber: 1.4g
Sodium: 227mg

Protein: 45.2g

Mean And Clean Italian Meatballs

(Prepping time: 5-10 minutes\ Cooking time: 20 minutes |For 6 servings)

Ingredients

- Salt and pepper to taste
- 2 tablespoons parmesan cheese, grated
- 1 teaspoon dried Italian herb seasoning
- 2 whole eggs, beaten
- ½ cup milk
- ¼ cup parsley, chopped
- 3 garlic cloves, minced
- ½ onion, chopped
- 1 pound ground pork
- 1 pound beef, ground

Directions

1. Take a bowl and add listed ingredients, mix well
2. Form meatballs from the mixture
3. Transfer meatballs to your Ninja Foodi Smart XL, select the Air Crisp mode
4. Cook for 20 minutes at 425 degrees F
5. Serve and enjoy!

Nutrition Values (Per Serving)

- Calories: 450
- Fat: 27 g
- Saturated Fat: 8 g
- Carbohydrates: 28 g
- Fiber: 3 g
- Sodium: 1273 mg
- Protein: 25 g

Everybody's Favorite Crusted Steak

(Prepping time: 5-10 minutes\ Cooking time: 10 minutes |For 4 servings)

Ingredients

- Salt and pepper to taste
- 3 tablespoons parmesan cheese, grated
- 2 tablespoons olive oil
- 2 pounds flank steak

Directions

1. Preheat your Ninja Foodi Smart XL in AIR CRISP mode for 5 minutes at 400 degrees F

2. Take your steak and brush them with oil

3. Sprinkle cheese, salt, and pepper on top

4. Transfer them to the cooking basket, cook for 6 minutes per side

5. Enjoy once done!

Nutrition Values (Per Serving)

- Calories: 577
- Fat: 37 g
- Saturated Fat: 8 g
- Carbohydrates: 23 g
- Fiber: 8 g
- Sodium: 688 mg
- Protein: 37 g

Perfect Onion And Beef Roast

(Prepping time: 5-10 minutes\ Cooking time:30 minutes |For 6 servings)

Ingredients

- 2 sticks celery, sliced
- 1 bulb garlic, peeled and crushed
- Bunch of herbs
- 2 pounds topside beef
- 2 medium onion, chopped
- Salt and pepper to taste
- 1 tablespoon butter
- 3 tablespoons olive oil

Directions

1. Add listed ingredients into a mixing bowl

2. Combine well

3. Pre-heat Ninja Foodi by pressing the "ROAST" option and setting it to "380 Degrees F."

4. Set the timer to 30 minutes

5. Let it pre-heat until you hear a beep

6. Arrange bowl mixture in your Nina Food Pan

7. Cook for 30 minutes

8. Serve and enjoy!

Nutrition Values (Per Serving)

- Calories: 320
- Fat: 17 g
- Saturated Fat: 4 g
- Carbohydrates: 11 g
- Fiber: 1.5 g
- Sodium: 185 mg
- Protein: 31 g

Coffee Lover's Steak

(Prepping time: 10 minutes\ Cooking time:50 minutes |For 4 servings)

Ingredients

- 1 and ½ pounds beef flank steak
- 2 tablespoons olive oil
- 1 teaspoon instant espresso powder
- 2 teaspoons chili powder
- ½ teaspoon garlic powder
- Salt and pepper, to taste

Directions

1. Insert the grill grate and close the hood

2. Pre-heat Ninja Foodi by pressing the "GRILL" option and setting it to "HIGH."

3. Set the timer to 40 minutes

4. Once it pre-heat until you hear a beep

5. Make the dry rub by mixing the espresso powder, garlic powder, chili powder, salt, and pepper

6. Rub all over the steak and brush with oil

7. Place on the grill grate cook for 20 minutes

8. Flip and cook for 20 minutes more

9. Serve and enjoy!

Nutrition Values (Per Serving)

- Calories: 250
- Fat: 14 g
- Saturated Fat: 4 g
- Carbohydrates: 6 g
- Fiber: 2 g
- Sodium: 294 mg
- Protein: 20 g

Juicy Beef Strip Steak

(Prepping time: 30 minutes\ Cooking time:15 minutes |For 4 servings)

Ingredients

- Salt and pepper to taste
- Dash steak seasoning
- 1 bell pepper, sliced
- 2 strip steaks, sliced into cubes
- 1 white onion, sliced into wedges
- 8 button mushrooms

Directions

1. Add grill grate to the Ninja Foodi Grill.
2. Close the hood and press the grill setting.
3. Set it to high. Set it to 12 minutes. Press start to pre-heat.
4. While waiting, thread steak and veggies onto skewers.
5. Season with steak seasoning, salt, and pepper.
6. Place on top of the grill grate.
7. Cook for 8 minutes.
8. Flip and cook for another 6 to 7 minutes.

Nutrition Values (Per Serving)

- Calories: 208
- Fat: 15 g

- Saturated Fat: 4 g
- Carbohydrates: 3 g
- Fiber: 1 g
- Sodium: 38 mg
- Protein: 14 g

Perfect Bourbon Pork Chops

(Prepping time: 10 minutes\ Cooking time: 20 minutes |For 4 servings)

Ingredients

- 4 boneless pork chops
- Salt and pepper to taste
- ¼ cup apple cider vinegar
- ¼ cup of soy sauce
- 3 tablespoons Worcestershire sauce
- 2 cups ketchup
- ¾ cup bourbon
- 1 cup brown sugar, packed
- ½ tablespoon dry mustard powder

Directions

1. Set your Ninja Foodi Smart XL to GRILL mode and select MED; set timer to 15 minutes
2. Add pork chops to the grill and cook for 8 minutes, flip and cook for 8 minutes more
3. Take a saucepan and place it over medium heat, add the rest of the ingredients and bring the sauce to a boil
4. Lower heat and simmer for 20 minutes
5. Drizzle the prepared pork over the sauce and serve

6. Enjoy!

Nutrition Values (Per Serving)

- Calories: 346
- Fat: 13 g
- Saturated Fat: 4 g
- Carbohydrates: 27 g
- Fiber: 0.4 g
- Sodium: 1324 mg
- Protein: 27 g

Fleshed Out Onion Beef Roast

(Prepping time: 10 minutes\ Cooking time: 30 minutes |For 4 servings)

Ingredients

- Salt and pepper to taste
- 3 tablespoons olive oil
- 1 tablespoon butter
- Bunch of herbs
- 1 bulb garlic, peeled and crushed
- 2 sticks celery, sliced
- 2 medium onion, chopped
- 2 pounds topside beef

Directions

1. Take your mixing bowl, add the listed ingredients
2. Mix well
3. Set your Ninja Foodi Smart XL to in ROAST mode and select BEEF
4. Transfer meat to cooking pan, let it cook until done
5. Serve and enjoy!

Nutrition Values (Per Serving)

- Calories: 320

- Fat: 17 g
- Saturated Fat: 4 g
- Carbohydrates: 11 g
- Fiber: 1.5 g
- Sodium: 185 mg
- Protein: 31 g

Premium Avocado Beef Meal

(Prepping time: 10 minutes\ Cooking time: 10 minutes |For 4 servings)

Ingredients

- 1 cup cilantro leaves
- 2 ripe avocados, diced
- 2 cups salsa verde
- 2 beef flank steak, diced
- ½ teaspoon salt
- ½ teaspoon pepper
- 2 medium tomatoes, seeded and diced

Directions

1. Take the steak and season it generously with salt and pepper
2. Set your Ninja Foodi Smart XL to GRILL mode, choose BEEF, and setting to Medium Rare
3. Transfer diced streak over grill grate and let them cook for 9 minutes, flip and cook for the rest of the time
4. Take a blender and add salsa, cilantro, and blend
5. Serve the steak with salt, tomato, and avocado
6. Enjoy!

Nutrition Values (Per Serving)

- Calories: 520
- Fat: 31 g

- Saturated Fat: 9 g
- Carbohydrates: 38 g
- Fiber: 2 g
- Sodium: 301 mg
- Protein: 41 g

Chapter 6: Snacks And Appetizers

Honey-Licious Asparagus

(Prepping time: 5-10 minutes\ Cooking time:15 minutes |For 4 servings)

Ingredients

- 2 pounds asparagus, trimmed
- 4 tablespoons tarragon, minced
- ¼ cup honey
- 2 tablespoons olive oil
- 1 teaspoon salt
- ½ teaspoon pepper

Directions

10. Add asparagus, oil, salt, honey, pepper, tarragon into a mixing bowl
11. Toss them well
12. Pre-heat Ninja Foodi by pressing the "GRILL" option and setting it to "MED."
13. Set the timer to 8 minutes
14. Let it pre-heat until you hear a beep
15. Arrange asparagus over grill grate and lock lid
16. Cook for 4 minutes

17. Flip the asparagus and cook for 4 minutes more

18. Serve and enjoy!

Nutrition Values (Per Serving)

- Calories: 240
- Fat: 15 g
- Saturated Fat: 3 g
- Carbohydrates: 31 g
- Fiber: 1 g
- Sodium: 103 mg
- Protein: 7 g

Well Prepped Yogurt Broccoli

(Prepping time: 5-10 minutes\ Cooking time:10 minutes |For 2 servings)

Ingredients

- 1 pound broccoli, cut into florets
- 2 tablespoons yogurt
- ¼ teaspoon turmeric powder
- 1 tablespoon chickpea flour
- ¼ teaspoon spice mix
- ½ teaspoon salt
- ½ teaspoon red chili powder

Directions

14. Wash the broccoli florets thoroughly
15. Add all ingredients except florets into a mixing bowl
16. Mix them well
17. Add florets to the mix
18. Let them sit in the fridge for 30 minutes
19. Take your Ninja Foodi Grill and open the lid
20. Arrange grill grate and close top
21. Pre-heat Ninja Foodi by pressing the "AIR CRISP" option and setting it to "390 Degrees F
22. Set the timer to 10 minutes
23. Let it pre-heat until you hear a beep

24. Arrange florets over the Grill Basket and lock the lid

25. Cook for 10 minutes

26. Serve and enjoy!

Nutrition Values (Per Serving)

- Calories: 113
- Fat: 2 g
- Saturated Fat: 0 g
- Carbohydrates: 12 g
- Fiber: 4 g
- Sodium: 124 mg
- Protein: 07 g

Simple Garlic Bread

(Prepping time: 5-10 minutes\ Cooking time: 5 minutes |For 4 servings)

Ingredients

- Salt to taste
- 1 Italian loaf of bread
- 1 tablespoon fresh parsley, chopped
- ½ cup butter, melted
- 4 garlic cloves, chopped

Directions

1. Take a bowl and add parsley, butter, and garlic

2. Spread the mixture on the bread slices

3. Transfer the bread inside the Ninja Foodi Smart XL cooking basket

4. Cook at 400 degrees F for 3 minutes on AIR CRISP mode

5. Serve and enjoy once done

Nutrition Values (Per Serving)

- Calories: 155
- Fat: 7 g
- Saturated Fat: 2 g
- Carbohydrates: 20 g

- Fiber: 3 g
- Sodium: 227 mg
- Protein: 28 g

Crispy Artichoke Fries

Prep Time: 5 min

Cooking Time: 13 min

Number of Servings: 4

Ingredients:

1 (14 oz) can artichoke hearts, quartered

FOR THE WET MIX:

1 cup almond milk

1 cup all-purpose flour

½ teaspoon garlic powder

¼ teaspoon black pepper, or to taste

¾ teaspoon salt

FOR THE DRY MIX:

½ teaspoon paprika

1½ cups panko bread crumbs

¼ teaspoon salt

Directions:

1. Press the "Air Crisp" button on the Ninja Foodi Smart XL Grill and adjust the temperature to 375 degrees F for 13 minutes.
2. Fold all the dry ingredients in one bowl and wet ingredients in another bowl.
3. Dip the artichokes in the wet mixture and then dredge in the dry mixture.
4. Put the artichokes in the Ninja Foodi when it shows "Add Food."

5. Dish out the artichokes in a bowl to serve when completely air crisped.

Nutritional Values (Per Serving):

Calories: 341
Fat: 4g
Saturated Fat: 0.5g
Carbohydrates: 36.4g
Fiber: 1.2g
Sodium: 547mg
Protein: 10.3g

Corn Fritters

Prep Time: 5 min

Cooking Time: 5 min

Number of Servings: 4

Ingredients:

1/3 cup cornmeal, finely ground

2 cups corn kernels, frozen

1/3 cup flour

¼ teaspoon black pepper

½ teaspoon baking powder

Garlic powder, to taste

2 tablespoons green chiles with juices

Vegetable oil, for frying

½ teaspoon salt

Onion powder, to taste

¼ teaspoon paprika

¼ cup Italian parsley, chopped

FOR THE TANGY DIPPING SAUCE:

4 teaspoons Dijon mustard

4 tablespoons vegan mayonnaise

2 teaspoons grainy mustard

Directions:

1. Press the "Air Crisp" button on the Ninja Foodi Smart XL Grill and adjust the temperature to 375 degrees F for 5 minutes.

2. Combine flour, seasonings, baking powder, parsley, and cornmeal in a bowl.
3. Put 1 cup corn with salt, pepper, and 3 tablespoons almond milk in a food processor and process until smooth.
4. Fold the corn mixture into the flour mixture until well combined.
5. Stir in the remaining corn kernels and spread this mixture in a pan.
6. Put the pan in the Ninja Foodi when it shows "Add Food."
7. Slice and dish out the corn fritters in a bowl.
8. Whisk all the tangy dipping sauce ingredients in a bowl and serve with corn fritters.

Nutritional Values (Per Serving):

Calories: 304
Fat: 30.6g
Saturated Fat: 13.1g
Carbohydrates: 21.4g
Fiber: 0.2g
Sodium: 834mg
Protein: 4.6g

Tofu Italian Style

Prep Time: 5 min

Cooking Time: 6 min

Number of Servings: 4

Ingredients:

1 tablespoon tamari

8 ounces extra-firm tofu, pressed and cubed

1 tablespoon aquafaba

½ teaspoon dried basil

¼ teaspoon onion, granulated

½ teaspoon dried oregano

½ teaspoon garlic, granulated

Black pepper, to taste

Directions:

1. Press the "Air Crisp" button on the Ninja Foodi Smart XL Grill and adjust the temperature to 400 degrees F for 6 minutes.
2. Combine the tofu with the remaining ingredients in a bowl and marinate for 20 minutes.
3. Put the tofu in the Ninja Foodi when it shows "Add Food."
4. Dish out the tofu when completely cooked and serve warm.

Nutritional Values (Per Serving):

Calories: 248
Fat: 2.4g
Saturated Fat: 0.1g
Trans Fat: 2.4g
Carbohydrates: 2.2g
Fiber: 0.7g

Sodium: 350mg
Protein: 44.3g

Original Crispy Tomates

(Prepping time: 5-10 minutes\ Cooking time: 5 minutes |For 4 servings)

Ingredients

- Bread crumbs as needed
- ½ cup buttermilk
- ¼ cup almond flour
- Salt and pepper to taste
- ¼ tablespoon Creole seasoning
- 1 green tomato

Directions

1. Preheat Ninja Foodi Smart XL by pressing the "AIR CRISP" option and setting it to "400 Degrees F" and timer to 5 minutes

2. let it preheat until you hear a beep

3. Add flour to your plate and take another plate and add buttermilk

4. Cut tomatoes and season with salt and pepper

5. Make a mix of creole seasoning and crumbs

6. Take tomato slice and cover with flour, place in buttermilk and then into crumbs

7. Repeat with all tomatoes

8. Cook the tomato slices for 5 minutes

9. Serve with basil and enjoy!

Nutrition Values (Per Serving)

- Calories: 200
- Fat: 12 g
- Saturated Fat: 4 g
- Carbohydrates: 11 g
- Fiber: 2 g
- Sodium: 1203 mg
- Protein: 3 g

Fancy Lush Baked Apples

(Prepping time: 5-10 minutes\ Cooking time: 10 minutes |For 4 servings)

Ingredients

- 1 teaspoon cinnamon
- Zest of 1 orange
- 1 and ½ ounces mixed seeds
- 1 and ¾ ounces fresh breadcrumbs
- 2 tablespoons brown sugar
- ¾ ounces butter
- 4 apples

Directions

1. Preheat Ninja Foodi Smart XL by pressing the "AIR CRISP" option and setting it to "356 Degrees F" and timer to 10 minutes

2. Prepare apples by scoring skin around the circumference and coring them using a knife

3. Take cored apples and stuff the listed ingredients

4. Transfer apples to Air Fryer basket and bake for 10 minutes

5. Serve and enjoy!

Nutrition Values (Per Serving)

- Calories: 150
- Fat: 5 g
- Saturated Fat: 1 g
- Carbohydrates: 35 g
- Fiber: 3 g
- Sodium: 10 mg
- Protein: 1 g

Mustard Veggie Mix

(Prepping time: 5-10 minutes\ Cooking time: 30-40 minutes |For 4 servings)

Ingredients

Vinaigrette

- ½ cup olive oil
- ½ cup avocado oil
- ¼ teaspoon pepper
- 1 teaspoon salt
- 2 tablespoons honey
- ½ cup red wine vinegar
- 2 tablespoons Dijon vinegar

Veggies

- 4 zucchinis, halved
- 4 sweet onion, quartered
- 4 red pepper, seeded and halved
- 2 bunch green onions, trimmed
- 4 yellow squash, cut in half

Directions

1. Take a small bowl and whisk in mustard, honey, vinegar, salt, and pepper. Add oil and mix well
2. Set your Ninja Foodi Smart XL to GRILL mode and MED setting, set timer to 10 minutes

3. Transfer onion quarter to Grill Grate, cook for 5 minutes

4. Flip and cook for 5 minutes more

5. Grill remaining veggies in the same way, giving 7 minutes per side for zucchini and 1 minute for green onions

6. Serve with mustard vinaigrette on top

7. Enjoy!

Nutrition Values (Per Serving)

- Calories: 327
- Fat: 5 g
- Saturated Fat: 0.5 g
- Carbohydrates:328 g
- Fiber: 2 g
- Sodium: 524 mg
- Protein: 8 g

Made in the USA
Las Vegas, NV
27 December 2020